"Travel is fatal to prejudice, bigotry, and narrow-mindedness, and many of our people need it sorely on these accounts. Broad, wholesome, charitable views of men and things cannot be acquired by vegetating in one little corner of the earth all one's lifetime."

-Mark Twain

For the Danney Brothers! Happy adventures in Italy! Ciao, Melanie + Tom

THE ADVENTURES OF Seymour & Hau

Italy

Melanie Morse & Thomas McDade

Illustrated by: John Soleas & Jon Westwood

Melanie A Morse

Thomas McDade

A **HONEY PUNCH** BOOK

More from Melanie Morse and Thomas McDade

The Adventures of Seymour & Hau: Morocco

The Adventures of Seymour & Hau: Ireland

Author & school visits available

Contact us at: info@seymourandhau.com

COMING SOON

The Adventures of Seymour & Hau: Malawi

The Adventures of Seymour & Hau: Cuba

Honey + Punch, LLC - info@honeyandpunch.com

ISBN: 978-0-9981725-1-4

Published by: Honey + Punch, LLC

First Edition

The Adventures of Seymour & Hau: Italy © 2018

For Aunt B, who told us to take that bus to Siena -MM

For Caleb, Charlie, Claire, Elliot, Jacob, Jasper,
Lucy, Luke, Mathew, Olivia, Remy, Ruby & Zak -TM

Thank you!

Grazie molto to the *Consorzio per la Tutela del Palio di Siena*! Thank you for your approval and for giving us permission to use the likenesses of the flags and clothing of the Palio, which are such a big part of the beauty and culture of this incredible tradition.

We would like to extend a very special thanks to Nicholas Bruttini for answering all of our endless questions and for his vast knowledge of all things Palio. Thanks to Barbara Canazzi-Mercurio & Massimo Mercurio for their help with editing, translating the Italian words, and for just being an awesome aunt and uncle. To Rosanna Mercurio for your generosity & hospitality in Siena. Also, to Rosanna and Massimo for being our real-life brother/sister duo! To Carlo Borgogni, thank you for the *Istrice* songs and for being our horse, and Lliana Borgogni for the delicious and inspiring food in Siena.

Thank you, once again, to our comma and edit goddess, Kathy Boyd! To our dear friend Natale Trigilio for lending her gorgeous face for our Rosanna. To Mom Patty for her edits and her perfect mama love and support and to Mom & Dad McDade for never missing a chance to be there for us. To Jacob, Elliot & Charlie Morse for being the kids behind the mischief and heart to our characters.

Finally, thank you to the people of Siena! Your passion and tradition is so amazing, and we are incredibly grateful to have been able to witness the Palio. We hope you enjoy our little story.

Italy

TABLE OF CONTENTS

INTRODUCTION

ME

Hi, I'm Seymour and I'm 11. I live with my mom and two younger brothers. I love playing street hockey, soccer and bass guitar. I used to be a regular kid until Hau showed up. I'm actually still pretty much like any kid on the planet, except that I get to go on wild adventures, face danger and help kids from all over the world out of jams. And by "jam" I mean "problem", not like the strawberry kind that you eat. Besides that, everything is the same, except that I'm hanging with a mega-galactic alien, and my closet smells gross.

Oh, BTW, I like to make lists. That's my thing.

HAU

Translation

My name is Hau. Take me to your leader earthling. LOL! My people think I need to learn some "life lessons," so they sent me to earth. Seymour is helping me to get back home. So far, the life lessons I learned are: I love Earth people, Earth food and Earth TV, especially The Voice, and Ellen Degeneres and Cake Boss. (I love fondant!) I live in Seymour's closet, and everyone here thinks I smell gross and say words wrong, but I think I smell ME-LICIOUS!

MY MOM

My mom's name is Helen, and she is the coolest mom on the planet. She doesn't yell... too much. I can't tell her about Hau, but she is getting suspicious. I heard her talking to my grandma on the phone, and she said, "That boy is acting so strange lately. He's always telling stories about different countries. It's almost as if he travels in his sleep." Can you believe that? I'd better be more careful. She also said, "... and his closet smells awful, I can't figure out what it might be." Let's hope she doesn't!

HOW I MET HAU

I swear, I thought this was spam until Hau stumbled out of my closet.

Incidentally, Hau loves SPAM, the food kind, not the junk email kind.

Hau's arrival - Inbox

To: Seymour
From: Morgeeta Dispatcher
Subject: Hau's Arrival

Seymour,
You have been chosen to help Hau regain his place on our planet. He has been sent to Earth to earn his way back. You will be sent on great adventures, face danger and help kids around the world. We cannot guarantee your safety but, you will be rewarded when your mission is complete. You will be tested and return tired but, no time will pass at home. We are watching and Hau's return home will depend on your success.

Best of luck,

Oruk
Dispatch Director
Morgeeta, Milky Way Galaxy

THE TELLUS

Hau has got this AWESOME little machine that he keeps in his pouch. It's called a TELLUS, and it "tells us" where we need to go and who we need to help. Get it? Tell Us. I'm dead serious, that's what it's called. It kind of looks like a cell phone with flashing lights all over it. It's connected to Hau's planet somehow. They know EVERYTHING that's happening on Earth. They are always watching us. Bizarre. There's a map on it, and a little black dot that blinks in the spot where we have to go. It also helps us with **The Leap**. There's a bunch of other buttons on it, too, but we haven't figure out what they do yet.

THE POUCH

OK, so Hau has this pouch. It's kind of like a kangaroo pouch but he can pull just about **a n y t h i n g** out of it—except maybe a baby kangaroo. They all have pouches on his planet.

I don't know EXACTLY what's in there. It's really random. I don't think even Hau knows, but I have seen him pull everything from a wheelbarrow to a "Kiss Me I'm Irish" t-shirt out of that thing. Now, if he could only pull out some soap...

THE LEAP CLOSET

It's really my bedroom closet. It looks like a normal bedroom closet: games on the shelf, clothes on the floor. The usual. However, when **The Leap** happens, the closet is totally NOT NORMAL. Once we shut the door, Hau pushes a button on the TELLUS, and everything turns the color of tie-dye. Then, it feels like you're on a crazy roller coaster ride and you land in a far away place. It is SO FUN! The Leap Closet is also Hau's bedroom... which is why it reeks.

ITALY & THE PALIO

Here's a little information about Italy and the incredible horse racing event that happens in Siena, Italy twice a year!

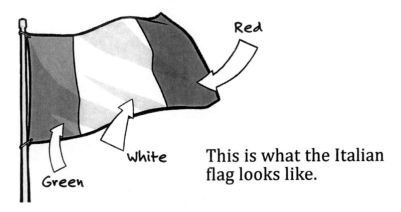

Red

White

Green

This is what the Italian flag looks like.

This is what Italian words looks like:

Sei incredibile!

That basically means, "You are awesome!" in Italian.

FUN FACT

Leonardo da Vinci and Michelangelo Buonarroti were both from Italy. These two guys were amazing painters and sculptors (among other things) and had a HUGE impact on art and science. Pretty cool, huh!

Official name of Italy: Italian Republic
(Repubblica Italiana)

Official flower of Italy: Lily

Location: Continent of Europe

Official languages: Italian

The money is called: Euros

Here are some other Italian phrases:

What is your name? --- *Come ti chiami?*

Nice to meet you. --- *Piacere di conoscerti.*

Hello --- *Ciao*

Goodbye --- *Ciao or Arrivederci*

Can I stay up a little longer? --- *Posso rimanere sveglio ancora un po'?*

How are you? --- *Come stai?*

Thank you. --- *Grazie*

Yes --- *Sí*

No --- *No*

STUFF TO KNOW ABOUT SIENA & THE PALIO

SIENA

There is so much to know about Siena and the Palio I don't even know where to begin!!

- Siena is a beautiful medieval city in the Tuscany region of Italy. You say it like SEE-EN-AH.

- Siena is made up of 17 different neighborhoods, and the neighborhoods are called *contrade*.

- Each *contrada* has its own emblem and colors.

  Here are all of the *contrade* and their flags:

Aquila (Eagle)

Bruco (Caterpillar)

Chiocciola (Snail)

Civetta (Owl)

Drago (Dragon)

Giraffa (Giraffe)

Istrice (Porcupine)

Leocorno (Unicorn)

Lupa (She-Wolf)

Nicchio (Shell)

Oca (Goose)

Onda (Wave)

Pantera (Panther)

Selva (Forest)

Tartuca (Tortoise)

Torre (Tower)

Valdimontone (Ram)

Aren't they AWESOME!?!

THE PALIO

- In Siena they have a HUGE horse racing event called **The Palio**. In Italian you call it *Il Palio*. It happens twice a year, and it is four days long. The fourth and final day is when the big race happens.

- The *contrade* race against each other, and who ever wins gets the glory! And also they win this hand-painted banner or *drappellone*. The banner is called...wait for it... *Il Palio*.

- The Palio is held in the town square called the *Piazza Del Campo*. They bring in dirt, make a track and then clean it all up after the race, only to do it again six weeks later!

- Each *contrada* gets to pick its own jockey but not its own horse. The horses get picked in a special lottery.

- Before the race there is a big parade called the *"passeggiata storica"*; which means "historical walk." The people who march in the parade dress in medieval costumes. Even the horse and the jockey walk in the parade!

- The people of the *contrade* will march the streets and sing the songs of their *contrade* during the days of the Palio. They are very proud of their *contrade* and excited for the race.

- To win, your horse has to run three times around the track and be the first to finish.

- Even if the jockey falls off, the horse can still win!

- If your *contrada* wins, it is THE BEST EVER. It means you are the awesomest.

I NIGHTLIGHTS

AHHHHHHHHHH!!!!!

I was hacky sacking out in the backyard with my friend Elliot when I heard my mom scream. There weren't even any windows open in my house so it was a REALLY loud scream. I raced inside. "OH NO! Did she find Hau?" I thought.

Then I heard it.

"SEYMOUR JOSEPH GET IN HERE!!!" she yelled.

Welp, there it was.

First Name + Middle Name = Trouble

"Please don't let it be Hau. Please don't let it be Hau. Please don't let it be Hau," I repeated to myself as I sprinted even faster.

My mom was in my bedroom yelling her head off.

Incidentally, your head does not actually come off when you are yelling your head off. It just means you're yelling really REALLY loud.

I finally reached my bedroom. My mom was yelling "WHAT IS THIS!! WHERE DID IT COME FROM?!?!"

She was standing in front of my closet. You know, my CLOSET, where Hau LIVES!

I tried to be cool, but too many words kept coming out of my mouth. "Oh, hey Mom. What's up dawg? Nice shirt. Did you change your hair? Would you like me to talk at great length about my school day? Um, is there a problem here?"

"What, ON EARTH, is THIS?" She handed me the red wooden mask I had been given on our adventure in Malawi. Phew, it wasn't Hau.

2

"Oh, that? I got that at a place where you, um, get things. I was saving it to give you for your birthday. Darn, Mom, now you ruined the surprise."

My mom looked shocked. Her eyes went into flying saucer mode. "You bought this for me?" she said. Then her face totally changed and she looked really happy and told me how sweet and thoughtful I was and left my room.

I closed the door and collapsed on my bed. I *was* planning to give that mask to my mom for her birthday. I just **happened** to get it in Malawi, which **happens** to be in Africa, which **happens** to be an adventure I went on with Hau. I can see why she would have freaked out. Even though the mask is AWESOME, it's kind of a scary thing to randomly find in a closet. I was just glad she didn't randomly find Hau!

"Hey, Hau, where are you pal?" No answer. "Hau?" I walked further into my room. He likes to jump out and scare me so I was preparing my brain for that. I grabbed my flashlight and shined it in the closet. There was a shaking, sweaty, smelly Hau hiding in the corner.

"What's wrong buddy?" I asked.

"Your mom came in here and said, 'Ew, what's dat smell,' and then she reached in the closet and so I had to make the mask fall off the shelf and then she screamed so loud it scared the nightlights out of me!"

"I think you mean daylights." I laughed. Hau laughed, too. He always feels better quick.

"I think you mean HEADlights," said Hau and he flew out of the closet and thwacked me in the head with a pillow.

PILLOW FIGHT!!! We were about to have the most legendary pillow fight when we were interrupted by that familiar sound.

2 LEAPING + LANDING

BBUUUZZZZAAAAPPPPT!
BBUUUZZZZAAAAPPPPT! BBUUUZZZZAAAAPPPPT!

It was the TELLUS, of course. And it was going off in Hau's pouch. Again. We froze the pillow fight in mid-air, like mannequins.

What happens next, always happens next.

1. I watch Hau's eyes pop open really big (like flying saucers).

2. He bangs his head on something random.

3. He searches through his pouch and tosses out random things that are in his way. Usually old food.

4. He says, "HA AH." (Did I mention he says things backwards sometimes?)

5. He finds the TELLUS and shouts out where we are going.

It's so super funny. You have GOT to see it sometime.

This time he shouted out, "We are going to Siena! Do you think we will "See ena" food there?"

I grabbed my backpack as Hau handed me the TELLUS. The little black dot was blinking on the country shaped like a boot. I'd know that country anywhere! We were going to Italy! SO AWESOME!

My teacher, Mrs. Adams, would always give us quizzes where we had to fill in the names of the countries, and Italy was always the first one I would fill in because the shape makes it easy to remember. It was my "gimme."

Incidentally, a "gimme" is something that is so SUPER easy that you may as well just get it without even trying. Like when you play mini-golf and you hit the ball so it's just balancing on the hole and you don't really need to hit it again 'cause everyone knows it will go in. "Gimme" can also be when your friend just got to a really hard level on your video game and he is starting to fail so you grab the controller and say "Gimme that!" so you can help him win. That kind of gimme is considered rude.

I pointed out the shape of Italy to Hau.

"Hey, Hau, see how Italy looks like a boot?" I said as I zoomed in on the Tellus and showed him the map.

Hau took a close, thoughtful look. Then he said with a straight face, "I get a kick out of that." He looked at me. I looked at him. We both started cracking up and headed to the closet for **The Leap**.

Hau stopped in front of the closet, grabbed a microphone out of his pouch and said, "It's SHOWTIME!" in his funny deep voice, and did a Michael Jackson tiptoe spin move. Oh, Hau.

It was time for **The Leap**. Best ride EVER!

Here's what happens. We go in my closet and shut the door. Then, it feels like we're on a roller coaster in the dark. The closet disappears and turns the color of tie-dye, like my Uncle Matt's shirts. We always hear this loud rumble, which is just Hau's stomach and not really part of **The Leap**. Then, it feels like you shoot up a hill and drop down another. Your stomach falls down to your toes, and then you spin like you're inside of a s t r e t c h e d   o u t   Slinky™. Then you're up and down, you shoot to the right, and then left and then swing upside-down. It's all over in about 2.5 seconds. It is SO FUN!

I really hope you get to try it sometime!

Although, you'll have to be prepared for the landing... it's always a mystery. I've landed on things that were soft, hard, super hard, sticky, stinky, squishy, slimy, wet and wiggly.

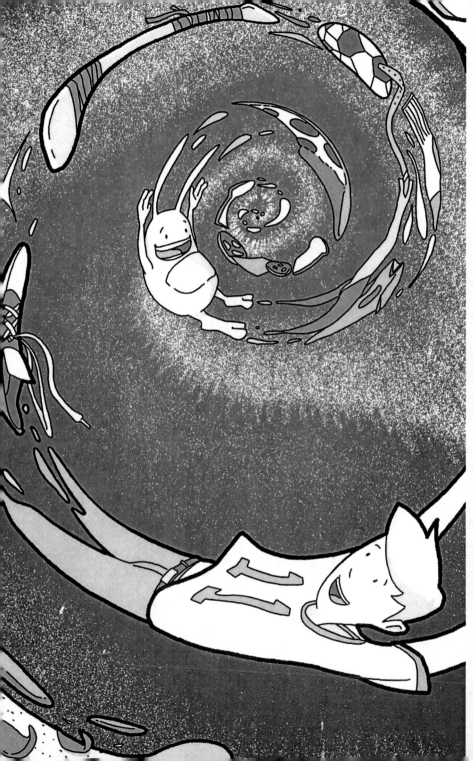

This time I landed in scratchy but soft. Hay. Lovely hay. Pain scale = 2. Not bad at all! I looked around. We were in a bit of an alley with very, very old looking buildings all around us. It felt like we were in the middle of an old castle town. It looked like this:

Suddenly I heard a sneeze. And then another. And then about 13 more sneezes in a row! I dug

around in the hay and pulled up a very sneezy Hau.

"I tink I'm ACHOO 'llergic to dis stuff," stated Hau, still sneezing. "It's pronounced 'AH-llergic' and it sure does seem like it!" I said.

"Got any bruises, Sey?" Hau asked between sneezes. He loves the bruise contest so much.

"Actually, no bruises this time! This hay was really soft," I told him.

"Me, too, I got none! We TIED for none!" said Hau.

So, usually Hau does his happy dance when he wins and his sad dance when he loses. But when we tie, we have a routine. Hau made it up. It goes like this:

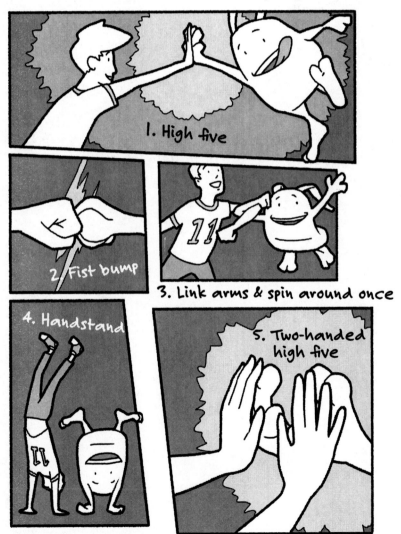

1. High five
2. Fist bump
3. Link arms & spin around once
4. Handstand
5. Two-handed high five

Hau was just asking to do it again when suddenly we heard someone coming. I shoved him back down into the hay to hide just as a young girl walked around the corner. She looked very worried. I had never seen someone look so worried. It's always the first kid we see after **The Leap** that needs our help, and she definitely looked like the one that needed our help.

3 CHOW

Her name was Rosanna. You say it like **ROW-SAH-NAH**. She had wavy dark brown hair that was almost black, and she nearly jumped out of her skin when she saw me.

Incidentally, jumping out of your skin just means you get startled or surprised. Not like your skeleton just starts running around the room.

It's definitely a surprise to see a random kid sitting on a pile of hay when you walk around a corner.

"*Ciao,*" she said, looking at me like I was bizarre. She looked a little older than me, maybe around 15 years old, and she was carrying a horse saddle.

"*Ciao,*" I said. In case you haven't figured it out

yet, "*ciao*" means "hi" and it sounds like "chow."

"*Posso aiutarti?*" she said in Italian. I had no idea what she said. I found out later she was saying, "Can I help you?" Lucky for me, Rosanna spoke English too, and she figured out pretty quickly that I didn't speak Italian. I was about to explain why I was there, when we suddenly heard exactly seven loud sneezes coming from inside the hay.

This is when I knew I needed to very quickly tell her about Hau. See, here is what always happens. There is no way around it.

1. Hau hides. In this case he was hiding in the hay. BUT, since we realized he is allergic, he sneezed his cover. (Get it, like "blew his cover," only SNEEZED... I crack myself up.)

   Incidentally, blowing your cover is like when you're playing hide-n-seek and you're trying to be super silent, hiding behind the couch, and you accidently sit on your dog's super loud squeak toy right

when the Finder walks into the room,
and the noise <u>blows</u> <u>your</u> <u>cover</u>.

2. I say, "Hi" and "Sorry" for whatever we broke. This time we didn't even break anything, we just made a few dents in the hay pile.

3. I tell the kid I'm here to help.

4. The kid is totally confused because how the heck did I know to come and help?

5. I explain about Hau because:

   A. If someone sees him too soon or they are not ready, they could run off, never to be seen again. Although that's never happened, it is a possibility.

   B. It's not nice to surprise people with a watermelon-sized, flying, bizarrely-shaped, eat-everything-in-sight mega-galactic alien. You need to give them some warning. It's only fair.

6. The kid totally gets it because kids totally get stuff that adults don't get.

7. The kid tells us the problem.

8. We get moving.

9. WAIT—first, we feed Hau. Then, we get moving.

Rosanna thought that Hau was "*adorabile*," which means adorable in Italian. That almost sounds exactly the same in English! Hau very much enjoyed being called "adorable."

Hau got right down to business. "Did I hear someone say "chow"? Where's the chow, pals?

Can someone please give me some of that chow that you were discussing? How about some chow right now?"

Hau went on and on. Rosanna and I looked at each other and laughed, but then her laugh quick turned back into a worried face.

She told us her problem.

She said that there is this HUGE horse race in Siena twice a year called *Il Palio*. She said her twin brother is one of the jockeys, and that the race was later that day but that he had just gotten stung on the arm by a bee shortly before we arrived. She said he is OK, but since he's allergic to bees, his whole arm swelled up and he can't move his fingers, and it will be a few days before the

swelling goes down. There is no way he can race. She said being chosen to be a jockey is a HUGE honor, and she feels so bad for him. She said she's the only one that knows, but any minute he was going to get picked up for the day's festivities, and he would get **eliminated** from the race!

I had so many questions I didn't even know where to begin. I decided we'd better go meet her brother and assess the situation.

Incidentally, "assess the situation" means to figure out what in the world was going on and what in the world we were going to do about it.

Hau and me followed Rosanna through the horse stables and stopped at a small staircase that led to a room above the stables. She told us we were inside the walls of the medieval town of Siena and that her brother was being guarded just at the top of the staircase, so we would have to sneak around the guards. She said that all of the jockeys get guarded during the week of the Palio.

"Why?" I asked.

"It's tradition," she told me. I learned pretty quickly that the answer to most of the questions about the Palio is, "It's tradition."

"Know what else is tradition?" asked Hau. "Giving me food. May I pretty please and thank you very much have some food? Ya can't break tradition, dat's what I always say."

Rosanna smiled. "There will be many treats and foods for you when we reach my brother. But first, maybe we hide you so we can sneak past the guards?" She pointed to my backpack. Wow, she really understood how we roll!

"Anything for food! I mean *for you*," said Hau with a smirky smile. He hopped in the backpack as quick as a wink, as my grandpa used to say... and winks are pretty quick!.

"I am allowed to go see my brother but you will not be," Rosanna told me. "Once I go inside, I will toss down a rope from the window, and you can climb up. I'll take Hau with me now so I can get him to some food faster." She peeked in the top of the backpack and smiled at Hau. I heard Hau whisper loudly, "Chow, Seymour! The food kind. HAHAHA!"

She put the backpack on her shoulders, and off she went. I could see the backpack bouncing around, which meant Hau was doing his happy dance inside.

4 TREE-TRUNK-ARM

I waited under the window. I could hear Rosanna speaking to the guards. I heard "*ciao*" again and then some friendly talk. They had just opened the door for her to enter when I heard Hau sneeze from the backpack.

Oh, no! *Had they heard?* I wondered. Just then I heard Rosanna do a bunch of fake sneezes VERY LOUDLY in a row. Then they all laughed and I heard the door close behind her. Phew.

Seconds later a rope dropped down, and I began to climb up.

Once I climbed in the window, we walked over to her brother who had the same worried face as Rosanna.

His name was Massimo. You say it like **MA-SEE-MO**. He was super confused. Rosanna quickly explained that we were there to help.

"We?" said Massimo. Rosanna told Massimo about Hau who then launched himself out of the backpack, landed on Massimo's lap and gave him a big slobbery hug and kiss. "How ya feelin' pal?" Hau is always instant best friends.

Massimo first looked shocked, then his face changed to amazed and then it went right back to worried.

"I'm terrible." He held up his left arm, and it was as big as a tree trunk! "It was after the *provaccia* (practice race) this morning. I was standing here on the balcony having a *gelato* and getting super psyched up to race in the Palio when I got stung by a bee. I think it wanted to share my *gelato*.

I will be fine after a few days, but whenever I get stung by a bee this happens. I'm allergic."

Hau gasped. "WHOA!! I'm 'llergic too!! To hay. Isn't dat cool? It makes me sneeze and I like it. So, tell me more about this *gelato* you were talking about."

This is like SUPER yummy ice cream, in case you didn't know.

It was then that Hau spied the large table FULL of food. It was so packed with delicious foods that Hau actually **fainted** for a second. Plates of meats and cheeses, bowls of olives, piles of pasta, baskets of bread with little vessels of oil for dipping. There was lasagna, pizza, fish, eggplant, salad, and big slices of tomato, and things I wasn't quite sure of. There were also desserts! Cakes, cookies, pastries, and even... gelato! Hau quickly woke back up. "Chow time?" he asked Rosanna hopefully.

"*Buon appetito!*" she told him, which basically means "Enjoy your meal!" Hau can understand every language, so he went right for it. *"Grazie molto,"* he said between giant bites of food all while dropping treats into his pouch. "Fer later," he always says.

Massimo and Rosanna both briefly suffered from pouch-shock* before snapping out of it.

*Pouch-shock: when someone sees Hau pull random stuff out of his pouch for the first time, and they can't understand how those things fit in there, and I can't explain it 'cause neither do I. But, this time they were amazed at how much Hau could put **in** his pouch.

Massimo smiled a tiny bit. Hau makes everyone feel better. I knew we had to hurry up and fix this, so I got down to business.

"If you can't race, what will happen?" I asked.

"Well, it's too late to change the jockey, so my *contrada* will be disqualified and we won't get to race. This will be so very disappointing for my *contrada*."

"What is a *contrada*?" I was so confused.

Rosanna gave me the lowdown as quickly as she could. Here is the list of what I learned.

> Incidentally, getting a "lowdown" is when someone tells you all the facts.

Here is the list of what I learned:

1. A *contrada* is like kind of like a neighborhood. The historic town center of Siena is divided up into different sections and they are called *contrade*.

2. There are 17 different *contrade* today, but there used to be lots more.

3. Here is a map of the town center and how the city looks divided up into *contrade*.

4. Each contrada has its own flag and colors, and they all have AWESOME names. You can read about them all in the beginning of this book. (Sneak over to the introduction.)

5. Il Palio is a race that has been running in Siena since the year 1656, and even earlier than that if you count when they didn't use horses. The contrade challenge each other in this race. It is a very important tradition.

6. Il Palio is run with 10 horses and each horse and jockey represents a different contrada. The 7 horses that didn't get to run the year before get to run automatically, and then three more are picked from a lottery.

7. The jockey's ride the race in traditional medieval clothing and they don't use a saddle!! That's called riding "bareback" on a horse. What if you were riding bareback on a BEAR's back? Double bear bareback?

8. The race is run in the *Piazza del Campo*, which looks like this when it's not set up for the Palio:

And like this when it is set up for The Palio:

9. The horse has to go around the track three times to win and that takes somewhere around 90 seconds.

10. If you win, you get a VERY COOL banner that has been specially designed by an artist and the winning contrada gets to keep it. It's VERY special to win. Also, this piece of cloth is actually CALLED *Il Palio*.

Also, on the day of the race, there is a huge parade and all kinds of traditions that the jockey has to participate in! So... we had some problems.

Specifically: **Massimo couldn't race in the Palio because of his bee sting tree-trunk-arm.**

The people from his *contrada* were picking him up and he had to leave for the *passeggiata storica*, which means "historical walk", in 15 minutes. If anyone finds out he can't race, his *contrada* will be disqualified.

If only we could find someone to take his place.

Just then I heard Hau say, "Ohhhh, I like dis shiny horse!! Look, Sey! Can I have dis for a souvenir? It's tradition."

I went over to take a look. It was a first place trophy for horseback riding. In fact, there were trophies and ribbons all over the room for winning horseback riding competitions.

27

"Wow, Massimo, you sure have won a lot of trophies! You must be a great jockey!" I said.

"Those are Rosanna's. She is an incredible rider." He said, very proud of his twin.

"WAIT ONE SECOND!!!" I shouted. "Rosanna, you can ride in Massimo's place! You're twins aren't you?!? We can just pretend you are Massimo, you can race, and then your *contrada* won't be disqualified!"

Suddenly there was a knock on the door. Rosanna shoved Hau and me in a closet just as someone walked in the room.

SIDE TRACK

They have five practice races called *Prova* that happen in the days before the actual Palio race. Tons and tons of people come to watch the practices! There is even a *Prova* on the day of the Palio. It happens in the morning and it's called the *provaccia*.

5 TWINS

I could only hear muffled voices from inside the closet and they left really quickly. When Rosanna opened the door I found out that they were just dropping off the jockey outfit for Massimo. It was SUPER cool.

Rosanna and Massimo happened to be in the *Istrice contrada*. You say it like **EE-STREE-SHAY** and it means "crested porcupine"! Their flag looks like this:

The jockey uniform was all striped in the *contrada* colors of red, white, blue and black, both the shirt (*giubbino*) AND the pants (*pantaloni*). And it came with a helmet that was also striped like the clothes. The helmet is called *zuccotto*.

The outfit looked like this:

"OK!" I said. "Rosanna, you have to put this on. You're going to have to race!"

"Me? I'm not prepared to race! What if people find out? *Istrice* could still be disqualified!" she said.

Massimo looked very seriously at his sister. "Rosanna, you know you can ride in the Palio. We have been trained the same way and everyone knows you're a better rider than me. I know you can do it. You're one of the best riders in all of Italy, maybe even in the whole world."

"Maybe even in da whole UNIVERSE!" added Hau, who was lying on the floor, exhausted from all the power eating he had just done.

Rosanna looked at all of us. "People will know it's not Massimo!"

"Well, let's at least give it a try. It will be up to Hau and me to make sure no one finds out. We are with you every step of the way," I said.

She paused.

"OK. I will do it for my brother, and I will do it for *Istrice*!" she exclaimed.

She grabbed the outfit and ducked into the closet to put it on.

She came out and stood in front of the mirror. Massimo stood next to her. They were the exact same size. The only difference was her hair was long and wavy and his hair was short and wavy. Lucky for us we had a helmet!

She tied up her hair as Hau clumsily hovered over her and set the helmet down on her head.

Now, standing in the mirror, you could not tell

the difference between Massimo and Rosanna, except for the small mole on Rosanna's chin. It was perfect.

Rosanna took a deep breath.

"Do you really think this will work?" she asked.

I nodded very positively, even though I wasn't super totally sure. It had to work. Massimo gave her a hug and a very encouraging smile.

"Wow, *sorella* (sister). If I had known you could look so much like me I would have had you take all my math tests." We all laughed, and Hau sang a bizarre song.

"I love math, yes I doooooooo, nine take away four is five, eight take away six is twooooooooooo!" I have NO IDEA where he comes up with this stuff.

Rosanna set her jaw.

Incidentally, setting your jaw means that you are VERY determined to do something and do it AWESOME. She was ready.

"Next time they knock on the door it will be time to go." Rosanna told us.

"OK, lower me back down the wall and I will follow right behind you. Hau, you stay with Massimo for now and keep him hidden."

"Copy that, brother." Hau smiled. He grabbed some cookies off the table and opened the closet door. "Right this way, sir," he said to Massimo. Massimo laughed and followed Hau into the closet.

Rosanna and I walked to the window.

"You got this," I told her.

She nodded. "Just stay close. The streets get VERY crowded," she said.

I climbed out the window and down the rope. As soon as my feet hit the ground, I heard the knock on the door to Massimo's room.

"We got this," I said under my breath as I raced around the alley to meet Rosanna.

6 BLENDING IN

I leaned nonchalantly against the wall, waiting for her to come downstairs.

Nonchalantly is super fun to say, **NON- SHA-LAHNT-LEE**. It means you just kind of hang out like you're cool and you aren't even up to anything suspicious.

The streets were crowded with people. Rosanna was right, it would be easy for me to blend in. But how was I going to stay close?

I looked around the alley and noticed that mixed in with all of the people in clothes like me, there were lots of people dressed up in clothes from what you might call the "olden days." I found out that they were historical clothes that are worn for tradition. The costume styles date back to medieval times, which is around 1600AD, during the Middle Ages. SO COOL!

Nearby was a group of kids, teenagers and grown-ups all dressed in traditional clothes of *Istrice*. They had on leggings that were stripped in the colors of *Istrice*, shirts that reminded me of The Three Musketeers and their shoes looked kind of like court jester shoes. Bizarre. Some of the kids had drums, and some of them had big giant flags they were waving and there was even a few guys dressed in armor! It was SUPER awesome, and I realized pretty quickly this group of *Istrice* folks were going to lead the parade, the horse and Rosanna all around Siena. I found out later that the people all dressed up are called the *comparsa*. You say it like **COMB-PAR-SA**.

They all began to line up just as Rosanna emerged from the doorway. Everyone was so excited that no one even thought for a second she wasn't Massimo. The people of *Istrice* began to sing the song of their *contrada*. It sounded like an

AWESOME chant. They began to cheer SO LOUD when the horse was brought out from the stable.

It was a beautiful shiny silvery grey horse with a white stripe down his nose and a white tail. He was dressed in the colors of *Istrice*, with a banner over his back and a tiny little stripped hat on. His name was Carlo and he looked like the COOLEST horse EVER. Rosanna climbed up. She looked excited and proud, even though I could tell she was a tiny bit nervous. She petted the beautiful horse to keep him happy and calm in the thick of the crowd. She caught my eye and gave me a nod. I didn't know how I was going to do it but I could not lose sight of her.

Just then, an idea popped into my brain. I needed to get my hands on some of those medieval clothes. I needed to join the *passeggiata storica* parade. I looked around and noticed that a few more *comparsa* were coming out of a doorway nearby. I rushed over and peeked in.

It looked like a museum filled with *Istrice* history. I scanned the room and saw Palio banners on the wall from past wins, and at the end of the room there were mannequins all dressed up in the traditional clothes! *Perfecto*! I would have to borrow some. I promised out loud to myself I would return the clothes as soon as I was finished helping Rosanna, then I snatched one of the mannequins and pulled it into a janitor closet with out anyone seeing. I quickly took off the mannequin's clothes and changed into the outfit, even the shoes and the hat. It fit like a glove! I grabbed a shield to go along with it, shoved my clothes in my backpack, waved goodbye to the mannequin and rushed back outside.

Incidentally, when something "fits like a glove", it means it fits perfectly awesome. It could be confusing if you have a glove on that was once owned by Andre the Giant, since that glove would probably be way too big, and NOT fit like a glove.

The drummers began to beat their drums and the parade began to march. I rushed back over to the alley and flung my backpack up over the balcony into Massimo's room and raced back out to the street. I slipped in with the rest of the *comparsa*, pulling the hat as far down over my face as I could, and using the shield to cover the rest of it, so no one would notice me. I snuck a look behind me at Rosanna who was now riding on Carlo, waving to the crowd that lined the narrow streets of *Istrice*. She caught my eye and I gave her a big smile and for a second I thought she might fall off the horse in shock. Her eyes went to flying saucers. We marched onward.

I had no idea where we were going. Suddenly we stopped in front of a church. Everyone got totally silent. ZERO talking. And then, we all started to enter the church. Rosanna got down off the horse and walked in. And you won't even believe what happened next... then the HORSE walked into the church!

7 HORSE LUCK

Inside the church everyone remained quiet. Rosanna had to keep the horse calm, and everyone inside the church was helping by being silent so it didn't freak Carlo out. Carlo was being a very, very good horse. He just stood calmly.

Suddenly everyone started smiling really huge and nodding and pointing and smiling more. Like the biggest smile you can imagine on someone's face. I couldn't understand what all the smiling was about.

Well, you may not believe me but it's TOTALLY true. Carlo had decided that now was the perfect time to, well, go NUMBER TWO. This time MY eyes went to flying saucers and my jaw dropped open.

I learned that it is considered excellent luck if this happens during the horse blessing at church.

It makes everyone SUPER pleased. If the horse wins the Palio, they actually even SAVE the number two in a museum. Bizarre. I looked over at Rosanna for some sort of explanation. She saw my face and simply mouthed the word, "tradition."

Works for me, I thought, still pretty shocked. I could not wait to tell Hau about this.

Incidentally, when you "mouth" a word it means you say it with <u>no sound</u>. Try it with your friends and see if they can understand you. I would suggest starting with something simple like "Hi" and then moving on to something more complicated like, "Did you know that Abraham Lincoln was the 16th president of the United States and he was 6 feet 4 inches tall?"

We all began to leave the church and, as soon as people were outside, the members of *Istrice* erupted in song. They sang the song of *Istrice* at the top of their lungs, and it sounded AWESOME.

They sang in Italian, of course. Later, I asked Rosanna to translate for me, and the words go something like this:

Sol per difesa io pungo

E' scriptorium bel Salome

Siamo dall'Istrice

Siamo dall'Istrice

Here is the translation in English:

Only in defense I punch

It's written in the societies

We are from Istrice

We are from Istrice

Pretty cool, huh?

8 TRIPLETS

So far, so good. Rosanna was doing an excellent job pretending she was Massimo. She continued to wave proudly, sitting up tall on the back of the beautiful Carlo.

The parade had begun, and we started out by marching through the streets of the *Istrice* neighborhood. Each *contrada* marches through its own neighborhood so that anyone who can't come to the Palio race can still feel like they are participating. Like if you're too old to walk, are sick, or if you have a broken leg or something.

Being in the *Istrice* neighborhood was especially AWESOME because everyone was singing and waving, and being really excited. Everyone was wearing the colors of *Istrice*. Black, blue, red and white were EVERYWHERE. *Istrice* scarves were tied around people's necks, and flags flew over every door, hung from every wall and decorated all of the shop windows.

Suddenly, something very peculiar caught my eye. I looked at a girl that looked EXACTLY like Rosanna. She was waving and jumping around super excited. She even had on the clothes Rosanna was wearing before she put on the jockey costume. It was totally BIZARRE.

Did Massimo and Rosanna have a triplet? I looked a little closer as we marched. She walked along with our parade. What was super EXTRA weird was that she had on MY BACKPACK. I had flung it over Massimo's balcony. I was so CONFUSED. I looked even closer at the backpack and I could see that something was bouncing around in there, just like Hau usually does. Then it hit me.

Normally when you say, "then it hit me," you mean that something suddenly made sense to you, or you discovered something. Like, I was going to brush my teeth, "then it hit me" that if I just wet my toothbrush, my mom would think I brushed. This time, I mean something actually hit me.

SMACK! Right in the kisser, as my grandpa would say. I was knocked to the ground. I wasn't paying attention to where I was going, on account of the Rosanna-looking girl with my backpack on, when one of the *comparsa* whipped me in the face with his flag by accident. He was just doing his job and throwing the flag in the air and I got in his way. Totally my fault. *Colpa mia.* My bad.

I had started a tiny little commotion because it made the *alfiere* (flag thrower) drop the flag, and that type of thing hardly EVER happens in Palio parades. The parade kind of stopped for a second and it seemed like all eyes were on me.

Rosanna saw what happened, and to distract everyone she pulled up on Carlo's reigns and he balanced perfectly on just two legs.

It worked! Everyone cheered! The flag guy quickly picked up his flag and we started to march again.

I was about to scramble to my feet but a grandma-looking lady stood in my way. Uh oh! I was in trouble.

Apparently the commotion was just long enough for an *Istrice* member to notice me and wonder what I was doing in the parade. She looked down at me and began to say something, VERY LOUDLY, in Italian.

She looked pretty nice and she reminded me of my grandma, who is super nice. But... when you are sitting in the street, after being smacked in the face by a flag, while in a parade you shouldn't be in, wearing clothes that aren't yours, and a grandmother-looking person is standing over you speaking loudly in a language you don't quite understand, you have to assume you are being yelled at. Right? I was pretty sure she was saying, "Who are you, and what in the world are you doing here?"

I started to slowly stand up and back away from her. The parade was marching on without me and I was going to lose sight of Rosanna if I didn't hurry up and get back in there. I was just about to spin around and sprint away from this lady when she grabbed me by the shoulders and looked into my face. She was super strong! I couldn't have moved if I wanted to! I thought for sure was going to take me to the police.

So far, so bad.

9 NONNA

The *passeggiata storica* moved on without me as this grandma-lady continued to stare at me. Then, her face made a huge smile and she pulled me toward her and gave me a giant hug. It was like the perfect grandma hug. Know what I mean?

Then, all of the sudden, I heard a familiar voice coming from behind me...

"*Ciao*, Seymour! It's me Massimo and that's my *nonna*."

Incidentally, nonna means grandma in Italian. But I bet you figured that out!

I knew she was a grandma! I thought.

48

Still trapped in Nonna's hug, I looked over and saw THAT GIRL THAT LOOKED JUST LIKE ROSANNA!! But, Massimo's voice was coming out of her mouth!

"Massimo?" I said.

"Yes, it's me!", he said.

I couldn't believe it! It was Massimo! He was dressed up like Rosanna!! Wig and everything! WHOA!!! I looked at his arm. It was still swollen like a tree trunk. Nonna let me go and then hugged Massimo. All grandmas like to hug, I think.

Massimo leaned over to me, pointed at Nonna and said, "She knows."

"What does she know?" I asked.

Massimo replied. "She knows you are my friend from America and you are helping us since I can't ride in the Palio. I had to tell her because she saw me and knew I wasn't Rosanna. Grandmas always know. She won't ever tell on us."

He looked identical

to Rosanna.

Nonna came over and gave me another big hug and said, "*Grazie, grazie!*"

Massimo explained to Nonna that we had to go.

She said, *"Sí! Sí!"* But then she stopped us and said, "Eat, eat, *mangia, mangia!*"

Mangia means "eat", of course. You say it like **MAHN-JAH**.

I asked Massimo later if she spoke English, and he said all she knows how to say is "eat." I was pretty sure if my grandma went to Italy the first word she would learn would be *"mangia."*

"Oh, no *mangia, grazie,*" I said. "We have to go."

Just then I could hear a muffled voice from inside the backpack that Massimo was wearing. *"MANGIA! MANGIA!* Me *MANGIA!"* Oh, Hau. He had been so quiet up until then.

"No, Nonna, we have to go," Massimo said.

With a smile and a kiss on both of my cheeks she said *"andiamo"* (which means "let's go"), but before we could leave, she reached into her purse and handed me a full bowl of pasta with a creamy white cheese sauce. Then she gave me one final hug and rushed off down the street.

I held up the bowl to Massimo with a *How?*

Huh? What?, look on my face.

Massimo shrugged. "I have no idea. She loves to feed people. Sometimes I'll run into her in an alley, and she'll hand me a plate of spaghetti and meatballs," he said. We laughed.

Bizarre.

We didn't have time to ponder any longer. We rushed down the stone street to catch the parade.

While we ran, we talked.

"WOW!! I can NOT believe how much you look like Rosanna! Well, actually I do believe it. I just didn't expect to see you! What are you doing out here anyway? Why aren't you hiding?" I said to Massimo.

"I'm sorry, I couldn't stand being stuck in the room when I could hear the parades outside my window. I had to come and see how Rosanna was doing and be a part of the Palio. I just could NOT stay hidden inside. It was Hau's idea to dress up like Rosanna. He saw how sad I was and told me he would find a way to help me. This was his solution," Massimo said.

Good old Hau. He always knows what to do. Well...almost always.

"Where'd you get the wig?" I asked. It was the perfect wig.

"Hau pulled it out of his pouch," Massimo said, matter-of factly.

"Matter-of-factly" means that you just say it like it's no big deal.

"Hau had a wig in his pouch??? That's a first!" I laughed. He hardly ever has EXACTLY what you need. This time, I guess he did. Hau's awesome!

"He had many wigs. Also glasses, mustaches and a costume of a red Power Ranger."

"Speaking of Hau. How are you doing in there buddy? How's Hau?" I asked toward the backpack.

Upon hearing his name, Hau unzipped himself.

"I'm great, pal! Did you hear Nonna talk about food? Should we maybe go back and find her? I would feel better if we found her."

Massimo pulled a powdery white cookie out of his pocket and handed it to Hau.

Hau smiled. "Ooooo, cookie!"

Massimo shrugged. "If I give him a cookie he stays quiet. I have a whole pocket-full."

I handed Hau the pasta with white cheesy sauce from Nonna. He slurped up the pasta, somehow managing to leave all of the cheese sauce in the bowl, then he stuck it in his pouch. "Fer later," he said, as usual.

"We've got to catch up with Rosanna! Massimo, can you show us where the parade route goes?" I asked.

Massimo stopped me. "First, you must change out of the costume. They will know you do not belong in the parade, and we will be caught. We already had a close call, but when the *comparsa* begin to perform there are many traditions and even some special acrobatic things to do during the parade in the *Campo*, and if you make a mistake everyone will know and it will bring suspicion to *Istrice*."

Campo? I wondered what that was. I made a mental note to ask when I had a chance.

Incidentally, a "mental note" is when you write something down inside your brain using your power of imagination and memory 'cause you don't have any paper.

Smart. OK. Time to change. I opened the backpack and asked Hau to hand me my clothes.

"Aw, MAN! I was using them as a cushion for my bum," he complained, and reluctantly handed them over.

Lucky for us, Siena is full of hidden awesome alleyways so I just snuck in one, changed, and we were back on track. I shoved the costume in the backpack so I could put it back on the mannequin later, and told Hau to NOT use it as a cushion for his bum. He agreed for a cookie.

We zipped Hau back in, and I put him on my back. We took off running down the *corso*, also known as the main street of Siena, turned about 27 corners and were right in front of a giant white marble church. It was AMAZING!! I could see the red, white, black and blue *Istrice* colors, and I knew we were in the right place. Phew!

10 BIRD LUCK

The church is called the *Duomo di Siena* which means the Siena Cathedral or Church. Most people just call it the *Duomo*. I got to go look inside and it is INCREDIBLE!! It looks like this:

HUGE, GIANT, pillars that are greenish-black and white marble! SO AWESOME! Also, there are tons of mosaics all over the floor. You are not allowed to walk on those parts, so when you go there don't forget.

> Mosaic = a whole bunch of colored tiles or stones that don't look like much when you look at them really close but when you step back they make up a whole super awesome picture.

There was an ENORMOUS crowd watching the parade, and people were gathered all over the

steps of the *Duomo*. There were streets coming in at every direction, and people never seemed to stop arriving to watch.

You see, at the steps of the *Duomo*, there is a big presentation by each *contrada*.

The whole *comparsa* marches past: the drummers, the armored men, the pages, the horse, the jockey, all of them! And the people with the flags throw their flags WAY WAY WAY up high in the air **simultaneously** (that means at the EXACT same time) and it looks SO AWESOME.

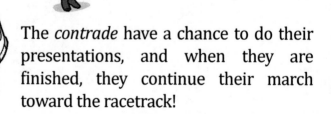

The *contrade* have a chance to do their presentations, and when they are finished, they continue their march toward the racetrack!

Rosanna was still up on the horse, nodding to the crowd, waving and looking exactly like Massimo. I called to Rosanna just as the flags were thrown in the air, 'cause when that happens, everyone looks UP! She saw me and looked relieved. I pointed to Massimo, and when she saw him she made a face that I had never quite seen before. She got the flying saucer eyes AND her jaw dropped to the ground AND her eyebrows went up as high as possible. She looked shocked, surprised, dumbfounded and baffled. **Shockprisedfoundedaffled**, I think they call it.

He waved and smiled and gave her two thumbs up. Well, one thumb and one tree-trunk-thumb. Hau poked his arm out and gave a thumbs up, too. Rosanna whipped her head straight forward so she didn't have to look at them anymore. I think it was so she wouldn't start cracking up.

We waited for the *Istrice comparsa* to finish performing and kept our eyes on Rosanna.

Hau began to complain.

"PLEASE, SEY. I want to SEE!! Get it? I want to see, Sey?" He laughed at his own joke.

I couldn't blame him. I opened up the backpack. There were SO MANY people around, hopefully they would all be too distracted to notice him. There were people nearby selling flags from all of the *contrade*. I decided to buy one to help cover Hau.

"Which flag do you want buddy?" I asked him.

"Dat's hard Sey, 'cause I really like ALL da *contrade*! Can I have one of each?" He looked hopeful.

"Sorry pal, right now you can only choose one."

"K-O. I will take the *Giraffa* for my first flag. Because it reminds me of your pal Jake who is really tall and I love that guy a lot."

I bought a *Giraffa* flag for Hau and wrapped it around his head so he could peek out.

Istrice had just finished performing in front of the church and began to head down a side street toward the *Piazza del Campo* where the race would take place.

The streets were so crowded I was surprised the parade could get through! But they did, with ease and grace and SUPER COOLNESS.

We began to follow and right at that exact moment Massimo got EPICALLY pooped on by a pigeon.

Epically = IN A HUGE MAJOR WAY, like GIGANTICALLY MASSIVELY ENORMOUS

It was in his hair, well his wig, all over his clothes and even on his cheek!! BLEGH!!!

My grandpa told me that getting pooped on by a bird is good luck. If that is true then Massimo just got good luck for the rest of his life, his kids lives, his grandkids lives, and his great-great-great grandkids lives. Horse poop, bird poop, I guess poop is good luck!

Massimo was smiling. "This is good luck, my *nonno* told me!"

I'm pretty sure grandpas are the same, all around the world.

nonno = grandpa in Italian, which is weird
'cause grandpa's usually say, "Yes, yes."
Get it?

"Ew, gross!" said Hau, and then he started to laugh so hard his *Giraffa* scarf fell off. I stuck him and his scarf in the backpack and zipped it.

Massimo laughed, too.

"OK, go get cleaned off. Hau and me will keep up with Rosanna. Meet us at the racetrack."

Massimo raced away to clean up, and Hau and me pushed our way through the crowd to keep up with Rosanna.

I I THE CAMPO

The parade was headed toward the *Piazza del Campo* – which is the name in Siena for the town square. Sometimes people just call it the *Campo*. This is where everyone in Siena hangs out, and this is where the Palio race happens!

The *Piazza del Campo* is one of the most beautiful town squares in the whole wide world. Remember, it looks like this:

There are restaurants all around the edge of the *Campo*, and it's an awesome place! There is a super cool fountain called the *Fonte Gaia,* which means "Fountain of the World."

During the Palio, it looks like this:

They bring in tons and tons of dirt to make the racetrack and when the Palio is over they clean up all that dirt and it's back to business.

The HUGE tower that stands up tall over the square is called the *Torre del Mangia* which means,

"Tower of the Eater." The very first bellringer of the tower liked to eat... A LOT, so that's why it's called that. I am not even joking. Maybe we could change Hau's name to *Hau del Mangia*?

The tower is connected to the *Palazzo Pubblico*, which is the town hall in Siena. These days it's still used for some government stuff, but it's also a museum and a theatre.

On super sunny hot days, the only shade in the middle of the *Campo* is the *Torre del Mangia* and people gather under the shade of the tower and move as the sun moves. It's funny 'cause the people make the shape of the tower shade.

Suddenly I heard a REALLY LOUD sound. It sounded like a cannon, and it meant it was time to begin the parade inside the *Piazza del Campo*. It's tradition. That sound means everyone has to clear off the track. When the cannon sound boomed through Siena, all of the pigeons started

flying all over. I covered my head so I didn't end up in a Massimo situation. Good luck or not. A lot of people were smiling and pointing at the big flock of pigeons. I heard that whatever *contrada* neighborhood the pigeons fly over is the one that will win. More tradition. But that one doesn't always come true.

I peeked into the *Campo* from the street.

Policemen and women had shut off all access to the racetrack, and they were beginning to clear all of the people off the track.

If you want to watch the Palio, you have to either watch from the middle of the track, or buy a seat around the outside of the track. If you're lucky maybe you can watch from a balcony that overlooks the *Campo*. If you watch from the middle, once you go in, you can't come out until the race is over and sometimes that takes hours and hours!

The streets were now so crowded you could barely walk through. Hau peeked out of the backpack with his *Giraffa* flag covering his head.

Rosanna and the *Istrice comparsa* headed toward the *cortile*, which is an area where the horses and jockeys rest until it is their turn to walk in the parade. It's kind of like a courtyard inside of a building.

Rosanna called me over.

"Seymour, wait for Massimo and then go and take your seats. I will be OK. The race will be soon. Wish me luck." She smiled and took a deep breath.

"Good luck, Rosanna. It is going to be AWESOME!" I told her. She began to walk away with Carlo.

Hau jumped out of the backpack and gave Rosanna a big slimy, squashy, slightly smelly hug. She laughed and hugged him back.

"Siamo dall'Istrice!" yelled Hau, remembering the song the *comparsa* had been singing though the streets. Do you remember what that means?

12 PRIMO TROUBLE

In no time at all Massimo was back and all cleaned up from that colossal bird poop.

"Nothing else can possibly go wrong, right Seymour?" he said, hopefully.

That's what I was thinking, too. Massimo was going to take us to our seats, and Rosanna was going to win the Palio. Simple. What could go wrong?

Our seats were amazing! All around the edge of the *Campo* were seats, like bleachers, stacked up in front of all the restaurants and shops that are usually open to the big town square. We were sitting high enough to see everything. It looked like there were a million people standing in the middle of the track and then thousands sitting in

the bleachers around the outside. We were lucky enough to be in the bleachers.

"This is incredible!" I said to Massimo. Scarves and flags waving, people singing the songs of their *contrade*, so many colors. *INCREDIBILE!*

Actually, only about 50,000 people can fit in the middle of the track, not a million, and then a few thousand more watch from the bleachers surrounding the track. It's still A LOT of people, but not a million.

Everyone seemed to know Rosanna. Massimo was waving, smiling and mouthing *"ciao"* to a lot of people throughout the crowd. No one seemed to notice that Rosanna was Massimo, not the actual Rosanna.

The policemen and women were still clearing people from the racetrack.

I sat there for a few minutes just looking at the

amazing view. Hau was being super quiet. He must have fallen asleep. I knew he would love to see this so I unzipped the backpack. Inside was a drowsy, sweaty, smelly Hau.

"Hey dude, I need a box of juice. Or maybe a cream of ice? It's hot!" Hau smiled.

It was hot, he was right about that! If I thought he smelled bad when he is clean he's worse when he's sweaty. Pee-yew!

He peeked out and he could hardly contain himself because as soon as his eyes adjusted to the bright sun the *Carabinieri* thundered by. The *Carabinieri* are old-fashioned policemen on awesome black horses. They come out right after the track is cleared of people. It's SO COOL! They gallop in a line and then all of the sudden they draw their swords and hold them out while they ride. Then they just disappear into an open wall.

"Do you hear that?" Massimo asked. All I could hear was the roar of the crowd and Hau saying, "Got any cookies?" But, I don't think that's what Massimo was talking about.

"What do you mean?" I asked.

"The bell," he said. I focused for a second. **Gong, Gong, Gong!**

"Yes, I can hear it. What is that?" I asked. "That's the *sunto*. It's the huge bell in the *Torre del Mangia*, and it will ring until the horses come out to line up for the race."

Just then Massimo turned toward an older man who was tapping on his sleeve. He was definitely convinced that Massimo was Rosanna.

I couldn't understand what he was saying, but

suddenly Massimo's face turned to stone.

Incidentally, faces don't actually turn to stone, it just means his face froze like he was shocked about something.

Massimo half-smiled at the old man and then turned slowly to me. He had an "OH NO!" look on his face.

"What's wrong?" I asked.

"That guy just told me that the Prime Minister of Italy is here," he said.

"The Prime Minister? That's awesome!" I replied.

"That's not awesome. Have you ever met a Prime Minister before?" he said.

"No, but it sounds cool," I responded.

"When the Prime Minister comes, she goes to meet all of the jockeys before the race," he said.

"Wow! That's lucky! Rosanna will get to meet the Prime Minister!" I said.

"You don't UNDERSTAND! When you meet the Prime Minster you must take your hat off out of respect!" Massimo practically shouted at me!

As I listened his words I could feel the blood drain from my face, and I was afraid my face would really turn to stone.

"UH OH!" Rosanna can't do that!" I exclaimed.

Hau just yelled "Hair problems!" from inside the backpack.

"We've got to get to her," I said.

"Yeah, follow me," Massimo said as he started to make his way down the bleachers. I was close behind, but we were traveling the exact <u>opposite</u> direction of everyone else.

Even though Massimo was like a halfback blocking for me, I felt like I was in one of those nature shows where the salmon swim upstream and jump up waterfalls to get back to where they were born.

Back and forth, in and out, saying "*Scusa, Scusa, Scusa,*" (if you couldn't tell, that means "excuse me"), as we made our way back to the *corso*. I must have said it 488 times myself.

Finally, we made it to the main street and wound our way over to the *cortile* where I had last seen Rosanna.

The gate to get into the courtyard was locked and guarded. I could hear the **clomp, clomp, clomp** of the horseshoes walking around in the *cortile* and the **gong, gong, gong** of the bell in the *Torre Del Mangia*. The race was ready to begin any minute! We needed to find a way in. I looked up.

"I've been here a bunch of times. We can get into the courtyard if we can just get through that window." Massimo pointed up, as if he was reading my mind.

"But how do we get up there?" he asked.

"Hau indeed," I thought. We needed all three of our brains on this one. The instant I opened the backpack Hau sprung out with a toy sword drawn, pretending to be like the *Carabinieri*. He flew super high. On the way down he grabbed onto one of the many flagpoles sticking out of the wall.

"What do you think, Hau, how do we get up to that window?" I said. With one hand still grasping

the flagpole, he dug his other hand into his pouch.

"Will dis work?" he said as he pulled a rope ladder out of his pouch. Massimo had gotten used to Hau pretty quickly, but when I looked over at him, he had pouch-shock all over again. Hau is amazing.

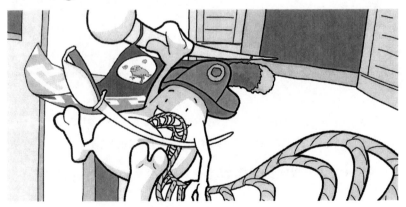

"*Si, incredibile!!!*" Massimo said.

"I got yur backs, pals," Hau said.

"Great, Hau! Can you attach it under that window?" I pointed.

"Surely, I can," he said, and followed that up with, "And don't call me Shirley." Then he cracked up. Really, I don't know where he gets this stuff.

Hau swung around on the flagpole like an expert gymnast, flinging himself from pole to pole until he reached the flagpole right under the window. He hooked up the rope ladder and dropped it down. We scrambled up, climbed in the window and pulled up the ladder just as a bunch of fancy black cars pulled down the alley.

"Oh, no!!" said Massimo, "That's the Prime Minister. Stall her!!!! I'll go find Rosanna."

Stall her? No problem.

13 WHITE CHEESY SAUCE

The fancy black cars lined up right under my window.

Stall, stall, stall... I had an idea on the tip of my brain, it just wasn't dropping into the thinking part.

Hau was walking in circles and worrying. When he worries, he gets extra hungry. I watched him dig around in his pouch for a snack. Suddenly he pulled out the creamy white cheese sauce Nonna had given us. Somehow, it was still warm!

GENIUS!

He was just about to pour it into his mouth when I grabbed the cheese sauce out of his hand and ran to the window. I dumped the whole bowl directly on the front window of the first fancy car just as people were climbing out. It looked EXACTLY like bird poop. It wouldn't give us much time, but bird poop slows everyone down for a minute anyway.

It worked! Every single person did this:

1. Froze in their tracks
2. Covered their hair
3. Looked up for pigeons (which were there because they are always there in Siena)
4. Quickly got back in the cars until they were sure all the birds were done

Hau looked like he might cry.

"But...Sey. My cheesy cheese sauce? My deliciousy creamy cheesy cheese. Why-eeeeee? Why on EARTH?!?" he wailed.

"It was for Rosanna. It was the only way, buddy. Now let's go! Hopefully that was a long enough stall."

Hau gave me a thumbs up. "I forgive you, but never do that again. Do I make myself clear?"

He grabbed onto the backpack as I ran through the halls and down the stairs to the *cortile*.

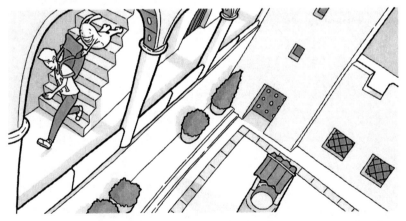

I could still hear the **gong, gong, gong** from the *Torre del Mangia* but the **clomp, clomp, clomp** had stopped. What happened to the **clomp, clomp, clomp**?

The stairs ended on the second floor, and I rushed to look over into the courtyard.

All of the jockeys were lined up with their horses standing perfectly quiet and still.

The Prime Minister and her security team were now walking though the gates. I was about to let out a yell to stall them longer, when I saw Rosanna take her place next to her horse. ***Oh no!!***

One by one the jockeys took off their hats and shook the Prime Minister's hand. She smiled and wished them each "good luck" or *"buona fortuna,"* as they say in Italy.

It was Rosanna's turn. She took off her *Istrice* hat, smiled, and shook the Prime Minister's hand.

"Had she cut her hair? Did she find a Massimo wig?"

I looked closer. IT WAS MASSIMO!!! He had his tree-trunk-arm covered with an *Istrice* scarf. Somehow they had switched back to themselves.

Amazing. Twins are SO COOL! The only problem was, they needed to switch back to each other. They were going to need some sort of a commotion.

A commotion is when you make a lot of noise that gets everyone all confused and slows everything down. It's similar to causing a ruckus.

If there is anything I am a professional at, it's a commotion. I'm also quite good at ruckuses.

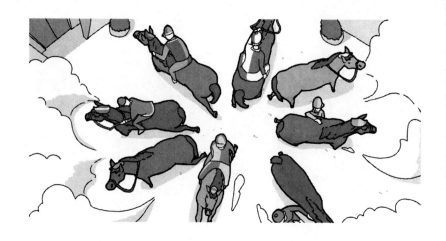

14 HOKEY POKEY

The Prime Minister finished shaking the jockeys' hands and headed back to her fancy black car.

The jockeys immediately began to mount their horses and head toward the racetrack.

Clomp, clomp, clomp. Gong, gong, gong.

I was about to create the biggest commotion ever when Hau began making exactly perfect horse noises. Whinnies and neighs. I'm not even kidding, he sounded EXACTLY like a horse. Can you make a horse sound? Let's hear.

All of the Palio horses stopped in place and began to pound their hooves on the dirt floor of the courtyard, creating a huge plume of dust. They refused to walk or listen to their jockeys.

Massimo knew it was his chance to switch back. He snuck off into a side room while the jockey's looked up, down, and all around. They were totally confused and couldn't see us because we were hidden behind a huge Siena flag. Some still sat on their horses while other's tried to climb on but the horses were only listening to Hau.

Hau continued to talk in horse-talk. All the horses formed a circle. Then they all put their right foot in the middle, and put their right foot out, and

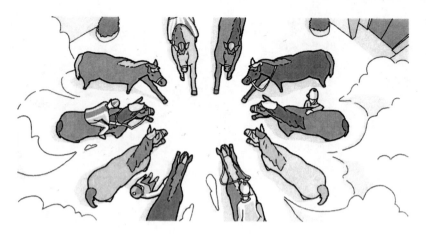

put their right foot in again. Then they shook them all about!

Hau looked at me. "Dat's what it's all about!" he sang.

Well, I never.

Hau was just finishing up the left foot part of the dance when we saw Rosanna, dressed as Massimo, sneak back into the *cortile*. She was laughing so hard at what Hau was doing with the horses.

"OK, pal. You can stop now," I whispered to Hau.

"Aw, man! I was about to do the backside in, backside out part!" he protested.

Just then Massimo showed up, dressed as Rosanna of course, and pulled a cookie out of his pocket. Hau immediately stopped making horse noises and then promptly told on me for wasting the cheese sauce and making it be bird poop.

Massimo laughed. "I'll get you more cheese

sauce. Nice job with the horses!"

The jockeys all suddenly regained control of their horses and walked them out of the *cortile* and toward the racetrack!

Massimo, Hau and I ran back to the window, dropped the rope ladder and hustled back to our seats in the *Campo*.

We sat down just as all of the horses were waiting for the starting lineup to be called.

15 THE LINEUP

The crowd was really going wild!

Massimo told me that it's best to get called sooner in the lineup because then you get to be on the inside of the track and that's a better chance at winning. You also don't want to be stuck next to your rival *contrada*. That's considered bad luck. The rival of *Istrice* is *La Lupa*. Tradition.

There is a special old machine in a room above the *Campo* that randomly picks the horses. It's got wooden balls inside that are the color of each *contrada*. A member of each *contrada* is in the room to make sure there's no funny business.

Incidentally, funny business is when you do something sneaky, like when your mom says not to eat any cake because it's for company but then you take a tiny bite and then smear the frosting around so no one knows there is a bite out. Usually your mom would not think this is funny, even though it's called funny business. Funny business is generally not funny.

Once the horses are picked there is a guy who brings the envelope down to the person in charge of the race. He holds the envelope WAY up high over his head to PROVE there is no funny business.

The *mossiere*, or the person that reads the lineup, began to read off the names of the *contrade* in the order they line up at the starting line. The crowd was LITERALLY on the edge of their seats. It got totally silent for a moment.

"*Bruco*!!" he shouted.

Caterpillar was first!

What luck! The people from the *Bruco* neighborhood were shouting and singing with joy!!

He continued to call out the order, and each jockey lined up their horse as they were called.

Nicchio (Shell), was next. Then *Onda* (Wave). The Shell and the Wave neighborhoods exploded with excitement.

He continued to call out the order.

"*Aquila* (Eagle), *Leocorno* (Unicorn), *Giraffa* (Giraffe)!"

Hau cheered for *Giraffa* from under his *Giraffa* flag.

Still no *Istrice*.

"*Selva* (Forest), *Civetta* (Owl), *Drago* (Dragon)!"

The crowd was on its feet singing and shouting! Flags waving, scarves waving!

I looked at Massimo. He had his hands on top of his head.

"I can't believe it! *Istrice* is *L'Ultima*!!"

In case you haven't figured it out... *L'Ultima* means the LAST one. That means when Rosanna runs in, the rope will drop and the race will begin. Usually the *L'Ultima* does not win. It's very rare.

All we could do now was hope for the best. Hau handed me some binoculars. That guy can read my mind sometimes.

I found Rosanna in the binoculars and she had her game face on. She was READY.

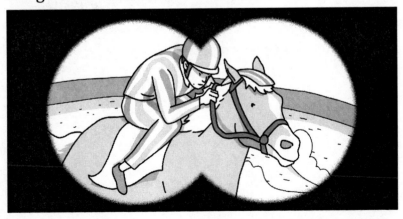

She waited with Carlo the horse until all of the other horses were lined up and settled down.

The crowd went silent again.

She waited a few more seconds, slowly leaned forward and BLAM!! Rosanna and Carlo took off toward the line of horses. The *canape* (rope) dropped and they were OFF!

The race had begun!!!

16 THE RACE

Rosanna was in last place as the horses bounded around the track. She looked like an expert rider, and I couldn't believe she didn't even have a saddle! Just after the first curve she started to overtake *Drago*. The people in the bleachers, still dressed in their medieval clothes, cheered loudly as she passed *Selva*. She was flying!

Rosanna moved over toward the inside of the track and passed *Civetta*. They were in the second loop now and she was getting ready to run around the dangerous curve. Carlo the horse ran like a champion and Rosanna crouched low. One of the jockey's had fallen off his horse and quickly ran off the track while his horse continued to run the race with no rider. These horses were SMART! (and FAST!!)

Incidentally, a horse can still win the Palio even if the jockey falls off. As long as the horse has the little special hat on when it crosses the finish line, it wins! Isn't that AWESOME!?!

Rosanna was full speed ahead, looking super focused, confident and FIERCE, as Massimo and I screamed and cheered as loud as we could. Hau could barely contain himself and kept leaping out of the backpack shouting, "*ISTRICE*!!!" but luckily no one noticed because everyone was too focused on the race.

She passed four more horses and finished the second loop in THIRD PLACE. One more loop to go. We screamed our lungs out and waved our scarves.

Racing neck and neck with *Aquila* and *Bruco*, Rosanna kept up the crazy fast pace. They were in the home stretch!!

"Hau, quick, hand me the binoculars!!" I yelled.

"Huh?" Hau looked confused.

"RHINOCULARS!! Quick!" Sometimes, I have to use his words for him to understand.

He quick passed them over and I found Rosanna through the binoculars. She seemed to be whispering to Carlo. He ran even faster! He was starting to pull ahead! The crowd screamed, Massimo screamed, I screamed and Hau was out of control!

Rosanna came around the final curve with Carlo a full horse length ahead. THEY WERE IN THE LEAD!! Running like the wind.

They were running so fast, in fact, that Rosanna's helmet flew off and her long hair bounced and blew and waved in the wind. **Uh oh.**

The entire crowd went silent and GASPED. Have you ever gasped? Try it. Open your mouth and breathe in loud. It's what you do when you are so shocked you can't even say a word, you can only breathe loud. Usually accompanied with flying saucer eyes.

Suddenly we heard the **BOOM BOOM BOOM** of the cannon as Rosanna crossed the finish line. She won. SHE WON!!!!

> Incidentally, when the Palio ends you hear three BOOMS from the cannon, not like in a running race where the winner gets to break past a ribbon at the finish line.

Normally when the Palio is over, everyone rushes onto the racetrack and begins to celebrate and cheer and carry the jockey on their shoulders and shout "*EVVIVA, EVVIVA!!*" Did you guess this means? "HOORAY, HOORAY!!"

This time everyone sat frozen in their seats. They could all see that it was Rosanna on the horse, not Massimo.

This was bad. This was very bad.

17 THE DECISION

Massimo went charging down off the bleachers and rushed to stand next to Rosanna. Rosanna still sat high up on Carlo and even though she knew she was probably in HUGE trouble, she had a GIANT smile on her face. She won. She won THE PALIO! Massimo looked up and gave her a wink. He was so proud of his twin and so grateful to her for riding in his place, even if they were both about to get a MAJOR "what for".

Rosanna jumped down off Carlo and stood next to Massimo as he pulled off his wig. The crowd continued to GASP and mutter and whisper and GASP some more, but it stayed surprisingly quiet.

What a pair. Rosanna in her *Istrice* jockey costume and Massimo with his tree-trunk-arm, in his sister's clothes, holding a wig.

A group of very official looking men and women scurried onto the racetrack. They seemed to come right out of the walls. There were 17 of them. I counted. One from each *contrada*. I couldn't tell what they were saying but they were speaking to Rosanna and Massimo VERY serious-like. Their foreheads were all scrunchy.

I watched through my binoculars. Rosanna spoke first, gesturing to Massimo's tree-trunk-arm. She used her hands a lot as she explained, and I

watched the official's foreheads get less scrunchy.

Then Massimo spoke up, holding up his still very swollen tree-trunk-arm, pointing to his sister and to Carlo.

The officials walked away from Rosanna and Massimo and got into a huddle, like a football team.

Then a tallish official stepped up to the microphone. She spoke in Italian and sounded very professional. She explained the situation to the crowd who were, once again, LITERALLY on the edge of their seats.

Massimo translated in my ear. She said:

"We have asked the *Istrice* jockey to explain why she is on the horse, and not the official jockey that was approved this morning to ride for *Istrice*. We asked why she deceived our beloved Palio race. She has explained to us that her twin brother was the approved jockey, and this morning, after the *provaccia*, he was stung by a bee and, because of an allergy to bee stings, he was unable to race. In order to keep the honor of *Istrice*, and to not disappoint their *contrada*, they devised a plan to simply switch places for the day. We have reached a conclusion as to the **validity** of the Palio race."

Validity = the state of being legally or
officially binding or acceptable

...in other words... Did *Istrice* win or did *Istrice*

get disqualified?

I held my breath. Hau was peeking out of the backpack, shaking like a leaf and taking slow huge breaths. "My nerves are shot, I need yoga!" he exclaimed. I have no idea where he gets this stuff but I knew he was nervous because he didn't even ask for a snack.

The crowd went silent. You could have heard a pin drop. Or a horse poop, which is what we did hear, loud and clear, 'cause of all the silence. Good thing I was holding my breath.

Rosanna and Massimo stood up tall and stared straight ahead, awaiting the official decision. I could tell they were both holding their breath, too.

The tallish official slowly opened her mouth and just said two words.

"ISTRICE VINCE."

ISTRICE WINS.

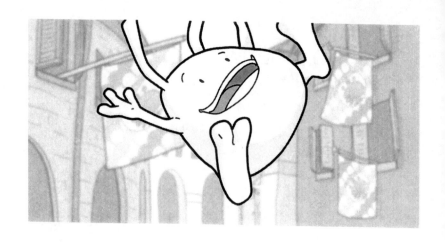

18 CELEBRATION

The crowd EXPLODED into cheers and applause!! Everyone rushed on to the racetrack cheering, waving scarves, hugging, crying, and singing!!

They sang the song of *Istrice!*

Sol per difesa io pungo
E' scriptorium bel Salome
Siamo dall'Istrice

Siamo dall'Istrice

All of the *contrade* were very proud of Rosanna and Massimo, and TOTALLY understood why they switched places for

Istrice. People of all the *contrade* said they would have done the same thing. Of course, *Istrice* was the most proud of all.

The crowd lifted Rosanna up onto their shoulders and marched her around. She found Hau and me and gave us a HUGE smile and a big wave and shouted "*GRAZIE SEYMOUR e HAU!!*" Can you guess what that means?

Hau blew her kisses, and me, well... I'm more of a thumbs-up giver.

Pretty much everyone in Siena headed to the church with the newly won Palio banner.

Know why? Tradition.

There were about a million and twelve *Istrice* flags and scarves waving. Hau and me marched along with the crowd to the church, singing, waving our scarves and getting hugged by everyone.

103

Hau had on the wig Massimo was wearing, so he kinda-sorta looked humanish.

Rosanna climbed back up on Carlo, with Massimo walking by her side. Before they entered the very super crowded church she stopped Carlo and reached down for her brother's hand.

"You deserve to be up here with me," she said very sincerely. He grabbed hold of her hand, she

yanked him up on Carlo with her and they **clomp, clomp clomped** into the church together.

A huge cheer and the song of *Istrice* continued as the people of Siena prepared to celebrate the Palio for the whole rest of the night.

19 ANDIAMO

It was time for us to go. Somehow we were able to help Rosanna and Massimo race in the Palio, and they even WON. It was a really great day. The sun was starting to set, and the *Torre De Mangia* was glowing and beautiful in the evening light.

The *Campo* was still full of people celebrating and singing.

"Come on Hau, we've got to get home."

"Aw, man!! I heard there's food tables! Food tables, Sey!!" he complained.

We were just about to duck in an alley and push the **LEAP HOME** button when we heard some familiar voices yelling, "Stop, WAIT!"

It was Rosanna and Massimo. They came to tell us goodbye. Rosanna picked up Hau and kissed him on both cheeks. He smiled his biggest and gave her a huge, slimy, slightly smelly hug. Then she did the same to me! I didn't mind so much, it's tradition. Massimo also gave us kisses on both cheeks.

"Thank you so much. You will always have *amici*

here in Italy. Come back to visit us soon. We have to show you *Roma* and *Firenza* and *Venezia* and *San Gimigniano* and *Capri* and all over Italy!" they told us.

"And you will always have *amici* in the United States!" I said.

Massimo handed Hau a large bag he had been carrying.

"This is for you, Hau. For letting me borrow your wig." Massimo smiled.

"FOR ME? OOOOOOO!! Tanks!! What is it??" Hau asked.

"All of the food from the food table," said Massimo.

Hau sprung up and gave him about 30 kisses on each cheek. Then he plopped the wig on Massimo's head and said, "You can keep the wig!"

Rosanna and Massimo waved as we walked away through the Campo.

Hau pulled out the TELLUS and pushed the **LEAP HOME** button.

The leap home is exactly the same as the leap that takes us all around the world EXCEPT... backwards. Like this:

1. You swing upside-down
2. Shoot left
3. Shoot right
4. Go down, then up (like a wave)
5. Slinky Spin
6. Stomach falls down to your toes
7. Drop down a hill
8. Fly up a hill
9. Hear a loud RUMBLE (that's really Hau's stomach)
10. Step out of the closet and into my bedroom

It is SO FUN! You HAVE to try it sometime.

20 HOME

We appeared in my closet at the exact same time we left home. *Back the same day we left*, as my grandpa would say. My room was the same as when I left it, and the closet still smelled like Hau.

"Something stinks!" said Hau. You know it's bad when Hau can smell it.

He dropped the Tellus in his pouch.

After an adventure I always ask him how the Tellus works. This time he put his hand over his heart, pointed one finger up to the sky and said, "Patience is bitter, but its fruit is sweet."

I stared at him. Where does he get this stuff?

Then he said, "Speaking of sweet fruit, got any grapes? They had lots of grapes in Italy."

Hau was right. They had SO MANY vineyards growing grapes in Italy. Rosanna also told us about beautiful beaches on the Amalfi Coast, and I really wanted to go to Rome to check out the Colosseum, and to Pisa to see the leaning tower and to Venice to ride in a gondola. I guess I would just have to go back someday! Italy was SO AWESOME!

AMALFI COAST

ROME

PISA

VENICE

I grabbed my *Guinness Book of World Records*™ and found out that the world's longest pizza EVER made was made in Italy. It was over a mile long and it took 250 people to make it! I wondered if Hau could eat a mile of pizza. What do you think?

Hau was snoring in my closet, snuggled up with the bag of food Massimo had given him and muttering...."Horses, flags, *Giraffa*, *ciao*, cookies, *gelato*, *tiramisu*, pizza, pasta..."

I wasn't sleepy, of course, so I grabbed a thumbtack and headed toward my map for my personal tradition. I stuck it in Italy, just above the middle of the country. Siena, Italy. Check.

I sat down on my bed and fell asleep in about 2.1 seconds, and I wasn't even tired! Isn't that bizarre!

Ciao! Goodbye!

THE END - *FINE!*

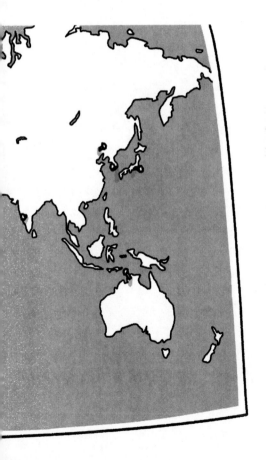

Melanie Morse and Thomas McDade currently live Buffalo, NY where it's actually pretty great. You should all come and check it out. When they aren't walking their super cute dog, Honey, or traveling with some particularly fun kids (also quite cute) they can be found producing and directing video projects and commercials with their company Honey + Punch.

seymourandhau.com
honeyandpunch.com

@seymourandhau
@honeyandpunch

More Adventures

CPSIA information can be obtained
at www.ICGtesting.com
Printed in the USA
FFOW02n2035290518
46923790-49187FF